W9-BAI-361

FAMOUS PEOPLE

George W. Bush

by Deanne Durrett

KIDHAVEN PRESS™

THOMSON ™

★

GALE

San Diego • Detroit • New York • San Francisco • Cleveland
New Haven, Conn. • Waterville, Maine • London • Munich

THOMSON

_™

GALE

© 2003 by KidHaven Press. KidHaven Press is an imprint of The Gale Group, Inc., a division of Thomson Learning, Inc.

KidHaven™ and Thomson Learning™ are trademarks used herein under license.

For more information, contact
KidHaven Press
27500 Drake Rd.
Farmington Hills, MI 48331-3535
Or you can visit our Internet site at http://www.gale.com

ALL RIGHTS RESERVED.
No part of this work covered by the copyright hereon may be reproduced or used in any form or by any means—graphic, electronic, or mechanical, including photocopying, recording, taping, Web distribution or information storage retrieval systems—without the written permission of the publisher.

LIBRARY OF CONGRESS CATALOGING-IN-PUBLICATION DATA

Durrett, Deanne, 1940–
George W. Bush / by Deanne Durrett.
    p. cm. — (Famous people)
Summary: Examines the early life of George W. Bush, his career as a businessman and governor of Texas, the controversial election of 2000, and his first year in office as president of the United States.
Includes bibliographical references and index.
  ISBN 0-7377-1371-2 (alk. paper)
1. Bush, George W. (George Walker), 1946– —Juvenile literature. 2. Presidents—United States—Biography—Juvenile literature. [1. Bush, George W. (George Walker), 1946– 2. Presidents.] I. Title. II. Series.
E903 .D87 2003
973.931'092—dc21

                                                                2002003260

Printed in the United States of America

CONTENTS

INTRODUCTION

From the Oil Patch to the White House

In January 2001, George Walker Bush became the forty-third president of the United States. Still a young man when he took office, George W. had experienced life in many different places in America. Raised in West Texas and educated in private schools in the East, he mixed small-town values with his Ivy League education. While working to complete his education, George W.'s summer jobs gave him experience in a variety of career fields. This included agriculture, ranching, the oil industry, politics, law, the stock market, and retail sales. In addition, he had earned his pilot's wings in the Texas National Guard, run an unsuccessful campaign for U.S. representative, put together a partnership to buy a major league baseball team, and was twice elected governor of Texas.

President George W. Bush signs a document in his office at the White House.

Bush brought to the presidency the management skills that had served him well in business and as governor. He also possesses Texas charm and sincerity, plus a sense of humor and compassion.

In his first year in office, a terrorist attack on September 11, 2001, pulled the United States into war. Bush rose to the occasion and most Americans believed him to be the right man for the job. They expressed this faith by giving him a 92 percent job approval rating in the polls. In years to come, historians will examine George W. Bush's policies and the outcome of his decisions. The full value of his presidency will not be known until many years after he leaves office.

CHAPTER ONE

Young Bush

George Walker Bush was born on July 6, 1946, in New Haven, Connecticut. He is the eldest of six children born to Barbara Pierce Bush and George Herbert Walker Bush. His siblings include Robin, who was born in 1949; John Ellis, who was born in 1953; Neil, who was born in 1955; Marvin, who was born in 1956; and Dorothy, who was born in 1959. In George W.'s early years, his family called him Little George and sometimes Georgie. As he grew older, he was called George W. or simply W (Dub-ya), his middle initial spoken with a Texas drawl.

George Herbert Walker Bush

When George W. was born, George Herbert Walker Bush was still a student at Yale University.

After graduation in 1948, the elder Bush moved his family to Odessa, Texas, where he began a career in the oil industry. In 1959 the family moved again, this time to Houston, where George W.'s father opened his own oil equipment and drilling business. After almost twenty years' experience as a successful businessman, George Herbert Walker Bush entered politics. He served in the House of Representatives from 1967 to 1971, and, beginning in 1981, as vice president of the United States under President

George W. Bush (far right) in 1964. As a teenager, Bush enjoyed spending time with his family in Houston, Texas.

Ronald Reagan. After the Reagan/Bush administration had served two terms, Vice President Bush was elected president. He took the oath of office on January 20, 1989, and he served one term as the forty-first president of the United States.

Barbara Bush

As first lady, Barbara Bush won the hearts of most Americans. Fulfilling the first lady's duty to support a cause, she chose to promote literacy. She made speeches and campaigned to promote the idea that everyone should learn to read. She also encouraged people to volunteer to help the less fortunate.

Young George W. Bush (center) had a close relationship with his mother, Barbara, and father, George Bush (posing in 1955).

In her younger days, Barbara Bush was a stay-at-home mom. During this time, her husband was building the business and often traveled. As a result, Barbara provided much of the parenting of the six Bush children.

George W. enjoyed a close relationship with his parents and was influenced by both. From his mother, he inherited his personality, sense of humor, compassion, and tendency to speak bluntly. His business sense and determination came from his father.

Tragedy Strikes

Tragedy struck the Bush family in 1953. Robin, George W.'s four-year-old sister, became ill. Medical tests revealed that she had **leukemia**. The Bushes took her to New York for the best medical care available at the time. Still, Robin died in October of that year. Seven-year-old George mourned the loss of his sister. Sharing this tragedy strengthened George W.'s relationship with his mother. He later said that this close view of death made him "determined to enjoy whatever life might bring [and] to live each day to its fullest."[1]

Love for Baseball

George W. later recalled in his autobiography that life went on after Robin's death. He wrote, "I filled many of my days with baseball."[2] He then went on to explain that he and his friends organized their own games and played baseball on the school grounds or the open area behind the Bush home. While he enjoyed playing the game himself, George W. also became a New York Giants fan. He memorized the starting lineup of the 1954 Giants team and poured over the first issues of *Sports Illustrated* to learn all he could about the players. His love for baseball would last a lifetime. As an eight-year-old child he could not imagine what lay ahead. One day he would be an owner of his own major league team, the Texas Rangers. Later, as president of the United States, he would step to the pitcher's mound and throw out the first pitch at Yankee Stadium in the third game of the 2001 World Series.

Education

George W. attended public schools in Midland, Texas. He earned good grades at Sam Houston Elementary School and San Jacinto Junior High. He also excelled at sports (especially baseball) and served as president of his seventh grade class. To this day, George W. calls Midland his hometown. However, the Bush family moved to Houston, Texas, in 1959. George W. continued his junior high years at Kinkaid, a private school in Houston.

In 1961 he enrolled at Phillips Academy in Andover, Massachusetts, where his father had attended. Sometimes called Andover, Phillips is one of the most esteemed preparatory schools in the United States. It is now coeducational. At the time the Bush father and son attended, however, it was an all-male school.

President George W. Bush throws out the first ball at the 2001 College World Series. Bush has loved baseball since childhood.

George W. mixed mischief with his studies and did not excel to his father's level of achievement. At an early age, he showed a talent for making friends and being a leader. George W. graduated from Phillips in 1964 and worked on his father's U.S. Senate campaign that summer. In the fall, George W. enrolled at Yale University. He graduated in 1968 with a bachelor of arts in history.

Texas National Guard

After graduating from Yale, George W. joined the Texas National Guard to become a pilot. Pilot training required a six-year commitment—two years of active duty (full-time service) while training and four

After college, George W. Bush spent six years as a pilot in the Texas National Guard.

years as a reserve (part-time service) Air National Guard pilot. During his reserve service, George W. flew an F-102A fighter jet. His duty was to help patrol and protect the U.S. coastline.

Back to School

After serving in the Texas National Guard, George W. decided to work toward a master's degree at Harvard Business School, one of the best business schools in the United States. George W. enrolled in 1973 and graduated with an MBA (master's in business admin-istration) in 1975. After graduating from Harvard, George W. visited his parents in China, where his fa-ther was serving as the ambassador for the United States. George W. then went back to Midland, Texas, to begin a career in the oil industry.

CHAPTER TWO

Businessman and Governor

When George W. returned to Midland, he was twenty-nine, single, and ready to make his fortune in the oil business. He had grown up in the "oil patch," as the local people called the oil field around Midland. The Bush family had many friends in Midland and in the oil business (many were very successful). These people helped George W. get started. In a short time, he made himself well known, and liked, throughout West Texas.

The Landman

At the beginning of his career, George W. went to work as a landman. As a landman, he searched the land records at the county courthouse to find out who owned the **mineral rights** to parcels of land around Midland. Based on this information, he helped negotiate deals

George W. Bush started in the oil business in Midland, Texas. He talks to oil-field workers there in 1978.

between oil drilling companies and the mineral rights' owners. These deals were called oil leases. The mineral rights' owner received payment from the oil drilling company for the right to drill for oil during a set period of time (sometimes several years). If the oil drilling company drilled and found oil, the mineral rights' owner also received a share of the income from the oil.

The Investor

George W. made small investments in oil drilling. His first investment proved to be a dry hole (no oil and he lost his investment). Drilling a second well near the first hole resulted in the discovery of a natural gas field. He wrote in his autobiography that the revenue from those wells "was enough to support me during my run for Congress in 1978 . . . and for the company I would build after my race [for election]."[3]

George W. and wife Laura campaign for Congress from the back of a pickup truck in 1978.

Laura Welch

George W. met Laura Welch in the summer of 1977. He immediately noticed that the young school librarian was "gorgeous, good-humored, quick to laugh, down-to-earth, and very smart."[4] They soon fell in love and were married a few months later on November 5, 1977. By then, George W. had decided to run for Congress on the Republican ticket. As a result, the newlyweds spent the first year of their marriage on the campaign trail. When the votes were counted in November 1978, however, the Democratic candidate had won.

Spectrum 7

George W.'s oil leasing business became a company he called Arbusto Energy. He expanded this company to include buying oil and gas leases and drilling for oil. This company became Bush Exploration. In 1983 Bush Exploration merged with another company, Spectrum 7, and George W. became the company's chief executive officer in the Midland oil fields.

The oil industry experienced a boom during the early 1980s. An oversupply of foreign oil, however, caused prices to fall sharply by 1985, and Spectrum 7 lost money. In 1986 Harken Energy bought the struggling company. The deal called for George W. to serve on Harken Energy's board of directors as a consultant in the business. Still, George W. had made friends and built a business relationship with his Spectrum 7 partners. Another, more successful venture would soon develop.

Vice President's Son

By then, George W. had become the vice president's son. The elder George Bush ran for president of the United States in 1980. He lost the primary election in June. However, Ronald Reagan chose him as his running mate. When Ronald Reagan was elected that November, George Bush became vice president of the United States. After serving two terms as vice president, in 1988 Bush ran for and was elected president of the United States.

Meanwhile, George W. and Laura established their home in Midland, Texas. They began their family and George worked to expand his companies. Their twin girls, Jena Welch and Barbara Pierce were born in November 1981, less than a year after George W.'s father took office as vice president of the United States.

George W. was involved in his father's political campaigns until his father was defeated by Bill Clinton in 1992. George W. developed some political ambitions of his own. He decided, however, that he would not become a candidate while his father remained in office. About the time the elder Bush was elected president, George W.'s career in the oil business ended. Within a short time, however, a golden opportunity came his way.

The Texas Rangers

When George W. heard that the Texas Rangers major league baseball team was for sale, he saw it as a chance of a lifetime. He contacted business associates

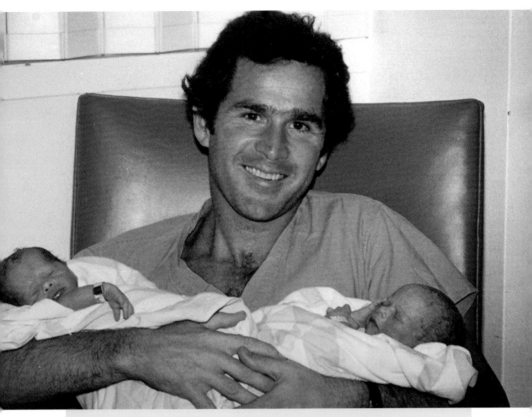

George W. Bush holds his twin baby girls, Barbara and Jena, moments after they are born.

and friends from his oil business days and pulled together a partnership to buy the Rangers in 1989. He later said that he pursued "that purchase like a pit bull on the pant leg of opportunity."[5]

George W. did not invest as much cash as the other partners. Instead, he devoted his time to managing the business and acted as spokesman for the team. Under George W.'s management, the team that had suffered a twenty-five-year losing streak began to win. This, along with a new stadium, inspired fans and made the

Alex Rodriguez of the Texas Rangers makes a play during a 2002 game. George W. Bush was once part-owner of the team.

team more valuable. When the partnership sold the team in 1998, George W.'s share was about $15 million, a tidy profit on a $606,000 investment. Now financially secure, the time seemed right for George W. to try politics again.

Governor of Texas

George W. Bush decided to run for governor of the state of Texas in 1993. Although George W. was born in Connecticut, he had lived most of his life in Texas and considered Midland his hometown. He had built a career in West Texas oil and owned an interest in the Texas Rangers. As spokesman and manager of the baseball team, Bush had become well known and liked throughout Texas. But Anne Richards (the sitting governor) was popular. Even George W.'s mother said he could not beat Anne Richards. Still, when the votes were counted in November 1994, George W. Bush was elected governor of Texas. Texans liked his policies and his approach to management. And, he drew the attention of the Republican Party leadership. Some of them wanted him to be the Republican candidate for president in 2000.

Texas governor George W. Bush speaks at a campaign rally in 2000.

"Compassionate Conservative"

During his campaign for a second term as governor, George W. began calling himself a "compassionate conservative." This means that he held conservative

Governor George W. Bush (right) and his brother, Florida governor Jeb Bush, speak to the media in 1998.

views about reducing big government and spending. At the same time, he pledged to provide help for those in need. In November 1998, Texas voters elected him to a second term as governor, although they knew he might seek the higher office. In January 1999, George W. Bush decided to seek the nomination as the Republican candidate for president in the 2000 election.

The 2000 Election

By the time George W. decided to enter the presidential race, he already had support from the Republican leadership. Although party support is important, it is not enough to be elected president. During his campaign, George W. would need to raise millions of dollars and persuade more than 50 million people to vote for him.

Campaigning for Votes

Candidates get votes by telling people where they stand on the issues and what they plan to do if elected. They meet people in person and speak at campaign rallies and town meetings. With his friendly personality, Bush was at his best while shaking hands and chatting with people.

To reach most voters, however, he needed television and radio time plus newspaper space. In addition,

During the presidential campaign, the Bushes visit a South Carolina elementary school.

successful candidates hire consultants and polling experts. This takes a lot of money. Stan Huckaby, a political consultant, estimated that a candidate for president in 2000 would need to raise at least $21 million by the end of 1999. According to an article in *Maclean's*, by June 1999 George W. was doing well. He had raised more than $36 million. Vice President Al Gore Jr. had raised $18 million by this time.

National Convention

By summer, the other presidential hopefuls, including John McCain (Republican) and Bill Bradley (Democrat) had withdrawn. George W. became the Republican nominee and Al Gore became the Democratic nominee. With that determined, the names of each party's vice presidential candidates would be the only mystery revealed at the national conventions. George W. Bush chose Dick Cheney as his vice presidential candidate. Cheney had served as secretary of defense under George W.'s father. Al Gore named U.S. Senator Joe Lieberman.

The Debates

From the end of August until November 7, the candidates campaigned almost nonstop. During that time, they agreed to three nationally televised debates.

Al Gore was thought to be the better debater. He had experience from his college debate team days as well as on the Senate floor while he was the senator from Tennessee. He had also debated in two success-

Laura Bush, George W. Bush, and Dick Cheney (left to right) smile proudly at the 2000 Republican National Convention.

ful presidential campaigns as Bill Clinton's running mate.

George Bush, however, did better than expected in the debates. He presented his views on the issues and came across as confident and sincere in his beliefs. And, after each debate, some analysts thought George W. Bush had won. The voters, however, would determine the real winner when they marked their ballots in November.

During the presidential debate, tensions rise between George W. Bush and Vice President Al Gore.

Electoral College

The presidential candidates and their running mates' names are listed on the ballot. It appears that by marking the ballot, the voter chooses the candidate. The U.S. Constitution, however, establishes that the **electors** from each state elect the president. As a result, voters are actually determining which political party will choose the electors (delegates to the **electoral college**). After each presidential election, the electoral college meets on the first Monday after the second Wednesday in December. At that time, the delegates elect the president and vice president.

Projections

November 7 finally arrived and American voters went to the polls. By midafternoon, media experts had begun analyzing **exit poll** results. This means that the media began compiling their own numbers after they asked people how they had voted. Soon after the polls closed, networks began declaring winners in each state's election based on this information. For the presidential contests, they began tallying the electoral votes state by state. This is called projecting the winner. Network **projections** are professional estimates but not an official count. In the past, most network projections have been accurate.

The Long Wait

Shortly before 8 P.M. eastern standard time (EST), all the major networks projected that Vice President Al Gore had won Florida's twenty-five electoral votes. A short time later, **precincts** began reporting from the Florida Panhandle. This portion of the state is in central standard time (CST), one hour later than EST. With the addition of these results, Bush gained votes and the media changed their projection to "too close to call."

A newspaper headline reads of the undecided U.S. presidential election of 2000.

About the time polls closed in the Pacific time zone, it became clear that Florida's twenty-five electoral votes would determine the president. About 2:15 A.M. EST, all the major networks declared Bush the winner of Florida's electoral votes. A short time later, Gore phoned Bush to concede. About forty-five minutes after the call, on his way to a rally in Nashville, Tennessee, Gore learned that Bush's lead was now only a few thousand votes. Believing he still had a chance to win, Gore placed another call to Bush. Bush responded, "Let me make sure I understand. You're calling me back to retract your concession."[6] That is exactly what Gore was doing.

Recount

Under Florida state law, the narrow margin triggered an automatic recount. Bush, however, held his lead. As it turned out, the counting machines rejected some ballots. In view of this, Gore requested an additional hand count of the ballots in four Florida counties where this had happened. These included Palm Beach, Dade, Broward, and Volusia. The count continued day after day. The totals changed and the gap between Bush and Gore narrowed.

Disputed Election

This set the stage for the most disputed presidential election in America's history. The dispute made its way from district courts to the Supreme Court. After a month-long dispute, the recounts were finally stopped

Florida election workers recount ballots, both by hand and by machine.

on December 9, 2000, by the U.S. Supreme Court. The court handed down its final decision on December 12, ending the dispute. In the final certified count, Bush received 2,912,790 votes and Gore received 2,912,253 votes—Bush won Florida by 537 votes. This gave Bush 271 electoral votes, a majority of the electoral vote, and that was enough to elect him president.

On December 13, 2000, George Bush delivered his first speech to the nation as president-elect. In the

George W. Bush is sworn in as the forty-third president of the United States on January 20, 2001.

speech, he said, "Vice President Gore and I put our hearts and hopes into our campaigns. We both gave it our all."[7]

Bush won the electoral college vote and was elected president according to the law set in the U.S. Constitution. Gore, however, won the **popular vote**. Many people were angry. Some felt Bush had stolen the election. Just as many felt Gore had tried to steal it. As a result, when George W. Bush took the oath of office on January 20, 2001, he became president of a divided nation.

CHAPTER FOUR

The First Year

No one had expected the forty-third president to face such a severely divided nation. They had hoped, however, that Bush would fulfill his campaign promise to work with both parties to solve the nation's problems. In recent years, the parties had not been able to work together for the good of the people. As a result, the House and Senate had not dealt with serious national problems such as social security and health care. Bush had hoped to reach out to Democrats from a Republican base, work toward compromise, and produce the needed legislation. The 2000 election, however, produced a Republican House of Representatives by a narrow margin and a split Senate.

When Bush took office, Democrats held fifty Senate seats and Republicans held fifty seats. The vice

The new president and his family had moved into the White House by February 2001.

president, however, acts as president of the Senate. In the event of a tie, he casts the tie-breaking vote. With a Republican in the White House, this gave the Republicans a one-vote majority. As the majority party, Republicans would be in charge of the major committees. This would help President Bush get his legislation passed on issues such as education, social security, Medicare, and tax rebates. As part of his effort to work with both parties, Bush encouraged bipartisanship in selecting committee chairmanships with possible co-chairmanships—shared leadership by both parties. The Democrats supported this idea.

The balance shifted, however, when Vermont senator Jim Jeffords, a Republican, changed his party affiliation to Independent. The Republicans now had forty-nine seats, the Democrats had fifty, and one seat was occupied by an Independent. As a result, a Democrat became Senate majority leader and Democrats became head of the major committees. Because of this shift Bush would have a more difficult time passing legislation to fulfill his campaign promises.

Inaugural Address

As one of his first duties, the newly elected president delivers the inaugural address. In his inaugural address on January 20, 2001, Bush shared his vision of an "America, at its best." He spoke of "an unfolding American promise that everyone belongs, that everyone deserves a chance, that no insignificant person was ever born."[8] With his likeable personality and

Government officials look on as President George W. Bush (seated) takes part in a signing ceremony the day of his inauguration.

sincerity, he reached out to every American. This speech delighted Bush's supporters and surprised his critics. It proved to be the first step in uniting the divided nation.

Uniting the Nation

It soon became clear that Bush planned to be the president of all the people, whether they voted for him or not. He met with leaders of the black community. He met with labor union bosses and Democrat leaders. He also extended invitations to Democrats in the House and Senate to meet with him at the White

House. In addition, he considered qualified Democrats for positions in his cabinet and other presidential appointments.

Experience and Skills

From his school days, George Bush had shown leadership ability and a talent for drawing people together. He developed his management style from his experience in the oil industry, as manager of the Texas Rangers, and as governor of Texas. He had learned to choose the best people for each position. Bush later said that in choosing his staff he looks for people "who are smart and loyal and who share my conservative philosophy."[9] Although Bush makes the final decisions, their judgment is a big influence. Almost eight months into Bush's presidency, people he had selected to fill high-level positions began advising him on how to lead and defend an America under attack. And, Bush's leadership skills would be put to the test.

Attack on America

On September 11, 2001, terrorists attacked the United States. Two highjacked planes flew into the Twin Towers of the World Trade Center in New York City. A third hijacked plane crashed into the Pentagon. And, heroic passengers brought down a fourth plane in Pennsylvania before it reached its target. More than three thousand people died that day. The attack also resulted in massive property damage and a devastating blow to the U.S. economy.

A sequence of images records the September 11 attacks on the World Trade Center towers.

War on Terrorism

In a speech nine days later, on September 20, 2001, President Bush announced that the evidence pointed to a terrorist group known as al-Qaeda and its leader, Osama bin Laden. At that time, he vowed to rally the world against terrorism. He pledged to bring the terrorists to justice. He said, "We will not tire, we will not falter, and we will not fail."[10]

After the September 11 terrorist attacks, America rallied behind the president. Congressmen and senators of both parties supported him in the war effort. In polls taken between September 11, 2001, and February 1, 2002, the American people gave Bush an outstanding approval rating.

State of the Union 2002

By the time Bush made his first State of the Union speech on January 29, 2002, he had banded with a group of countries to fight terrorism and wipe out al-Qaeda in Afghanistan. Still, bin Laden had not been found and Bush vowed to continue the war. He said, "Our war against terror is only beginning. . . . We will win this war, we will protect our homeland and we will revive our economy."[11]

A video clip shows Osama bin Laden riding a horse in Afghanistan in 1998.

The president and first lady wave as they board Air Force One *in 2002.*

In the first year of his presidency, Bush worked to become the president of all Americans. He pulled Congress together to pass his tax cut and education legislation. He did well as the leader of an America under attack. In little more than an hour on September 11, 2001, the focus of the Bush presidency changed in a way no one could have predicted. And there is no way to predict what the remaining three years of his term will bring or how historians will rate the Bush presidency. For now, George W. Bush is the president of a nation united against a terrorist enemy. Still, he faces the challenges of **partisan politics**, a shaky economy, and another election, if he decides to run.

NOTES

Chapter One: Young Bush
1. George W. Bush, *A Charge to Keep*. New York: William Morrow, 1999, p. 15.
2. Bush, *A Charge to Keep*, p. 15.

Chapter Two: Businessman and Governor
3. Bush, *A Charge to Keep*, p. 62.
4. Bush, *A Charge to Keep*, p. 79.
5. Bush, *A Charge to Keep*, p. 198.

Chapter Three: The 2000 Election
6. "How We Got Here: A Timeline of the Florida Recount," www.cnn.com. *Allpolitics.com with Time Election 2000.*
7. George W. Bush, speech, December 13, 2000, www.cnn. com.

Chapter Four: The First Year
8. George W. Bush, "Inaugural Address," January 20, 2001, www.whitehouse.gov.
9. Bush, *A Charge to Keep*, p. 104.
10. George W. Bush, "Address to a Joint Session of

Congress and the American People," September 20, 2001.

11. George W. Bush, "State of the Union Address," January 29, 2002. www.whitehouse.gov.

GLOSSARY

electoral college: A group of electors from each state whose votes actually elect the president of the United States.

electors: Delegates from each state who participate in the electoral college.

exit polls: A poll taken by the media of voters leaving the voting place; it is usually used to predict the winners.

leukemia: Cancer of the blood.

mineral rights: The owner of the minerals and oil in a specific parcel of land. (A person may own the land but not the mineral rights.)

popular vote: The votes cast for a candidate or electors for that candidate.

partisan politics: When members of one major political party unite against the other major party in supporting an issue or voting.

precinct: A voting district.

projection: An estimate of what the total count will be, based on a percentage.

For Further Exploration

Books

Dan Gutman, *Landslide!: A Kid's Guide to the U.S. Elections.* New York: Aladdin Paperbacks, 2000. Written in a question-and-answer format, this book explains the U.S. democratic process.

Miles Harvey, *Presidential Elections.* Danbury, CT: Childrens Press, 1995. A thirty-two-page picture book that examines the election process. Ideal for readers ages nine through twelve.

Martha S. Hewson, *The Electoral College (Your Government—How It Works).* Broomall, PA: Chelsea House, 2002. A brand new book that examines the presidential election process and the electoral college.

Judith St. George, *So You Want to Be President?* New York: Philomel Books, 2000. A fun read packed with interesting facts about presidents.

Website

White House Kids (www.whitehousekids.gov). A fun biography of George W. Bush. It includes answers to questions kids might ask such as "What is your favorite ice cream flavor?"

INDEX

PICTURE CREDITS

Cover photo: © Joseph Sohm, ChromoSohm
  Inc./CORBIS

© AFP/CORBIS, 5, 28, 29, 31, 36, 39

© Associated Press, AP, 11, 20, 22, 25, 27, 40

© Associated Press, George Bush Presidential
  Library, 9, 12, 15, 17, 19

© Craig Aurness/CORBIS, 34

© CORBIS, 7

© Wally McNamee/CORBIS, 32

© Reuters NewMedia Inc./CORBIS, 21, 38

ABOUT THE AUTHOR

Deanne Durrett has been writing nonfiction books for kids since 1993. She writes on a variety of subjects, but her favorites are biographies. She loves research because, like life, it is an adventure filled with discovery. She and her husband, Dan, live in Arizona with Einstein (a mini schnauzer) and Willie (an Abyssinian cat).